Evening
In
Sydney
Harbor

FACES AND PLACES

AUSTRALIA

BY MARY BERENDES

THE CHILD'S WORLD®, INC.

Area: About 3 million square miles—
a little smaller than the United States.

Population: About 18 million people.

Capital City: Canberra.

Other Important Cities: Sydney, Melbourne, Brisbane, Perth, Adelaide.

Money: The Australian dollar. An Australian dollar is divided into 100 cents.

National Language: English.

National Song: "Advance Australia Fair" A special song is also played for Queen Elizabeth II. It is called "God Save The Queen."

National Holiday: Australia Day, January 26.

National Flag: Blue with the flag of Great Britain in the upper left corner. There are also lots of stars on the flag. The biggest star stands for Australia. The smaller stars represent the *Southern Cross*, a group of stars in the sky.

Head of Government: Prime Minister John Winston Howard.

Chief of State: Queen Elizabeth II of Great Britain.

Library of Congress Cataloging-in-Publication Data
Berendes, Mary.
Australia / by Mary Berendes.
Series: "Faces and Places".
p. cm.
Includes index.
Summary: Describes the geography, history, people, and customs of the only country that is also a continent.
ISBN 1-56766-513-6 (library : reinforced : alk. paper)

1. Australia — Juvenile literature.
[1. Australia.] I. Title.

DU96.B47 1998
994 — dc21
97-40650
CIP
AC

GRAPHIC DESIGN
Robert A. Honey, Seattle

PHOTO RESEARCH
James R. Rothaus / James R. Rothaus & Associates

ELECTRONIC PRE–PRESS PRODUCTION
Robert E. Bonaker / Graphic Design & Consulting Co.

PHOTOGRAPHY
Cover photo: Young Girl Holding Wallaby
by Michael Yamashita/Corbis

Table of Contents

CHAPTER	PAGE
Where is Australia?	6
The Land	9
Plants and Animals	10
Long Ago	13
Australia Today	14
The People	17
City Life and Country Life	18
Schools and Language	21
Work	22
Food	25
Pastimes	26
Holidays	29
Index & Glossary	32

From high above, Earth looks like a big, blue ball. But if you look closely, you can see many things. The blue patches are really oceans and seas. There are also huge brown and green patches. These are land areas called **continents**. Australia is a continent. It lies between the Indian and South Pacific Oceans.

Western Hemisphere

Eastern Hemisphere

Australia (white) is in the east and U.S.A. (green) is in the west

Some of the world's continents are made up of different countries. But Australia is different.

Only one country can be found there—Australia! Australia is the only continent that is also a country.

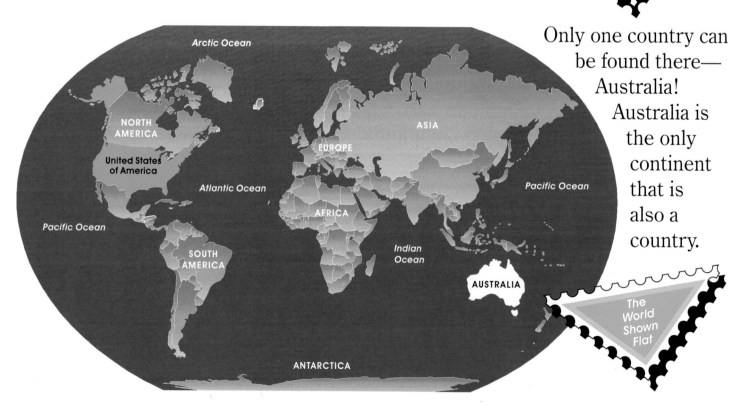

Arctic Ocean

NORTH AMERICA

United States of America

Atlantic Ocean

Pacific Ocean

ASIA

EUROPE

Pacific Ocean

AFRICA

SOUTH AMERICA

Indian Ocean

AUSTRALIA

The World Shown Flat

ANTARCTICA

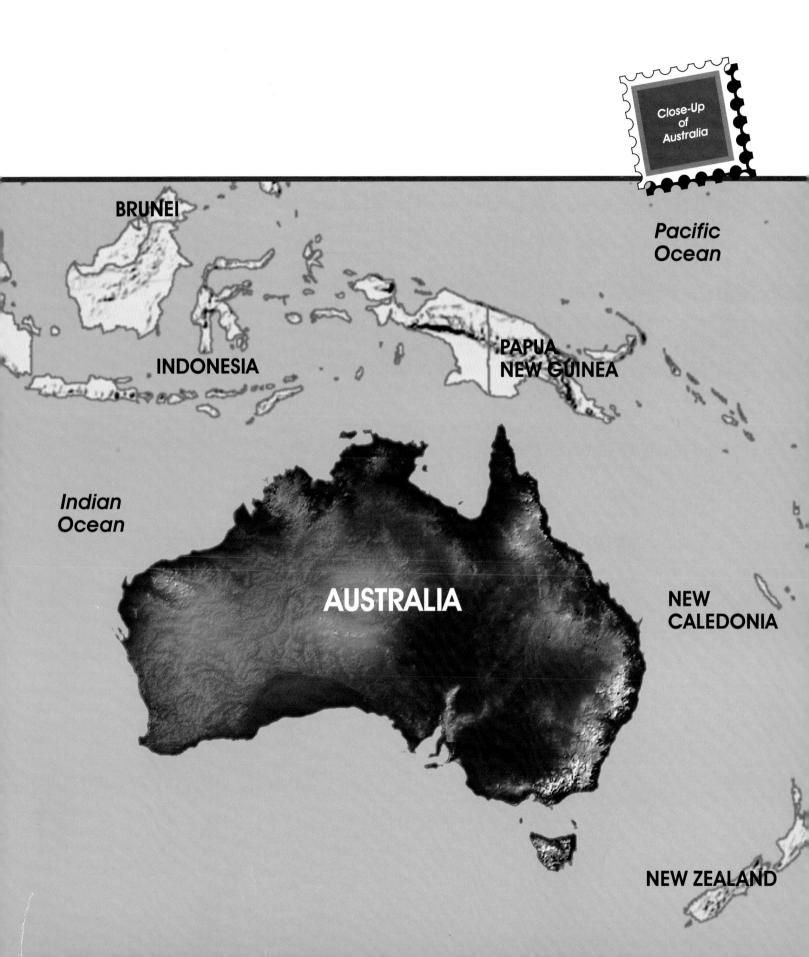

BRUNEI

*Pacific
Ocean*

INDONESIA

PAPUA
NEW GUINEA

*Indian
Ocean*

AUSTRALIA

NEW
CALEDONIA

NEW ZEALAND

Three Sisters
In Blue
Mountian
National
Park

Cabourg
Peninsula

Great Barrier Reef

+Ayers
Rock

Pinnacles
Desert

BLUE
MOUNTAINS

Sydney

Paul A. Souders/© Corbis

The Land

ADMIT ONE   ADMIT ONE

Pinnacles Desert

Most of Australia is low, flat, and dry. Many areas are covered with short bushes and grasses. In some places, there is nothing but sandy desert. But there are also low mountains and flat areas called **plateaus**. A plateau is an area of land that is higher than the lands around it. Some of Australia's plateaus have rich soil that is good for farming. Others are covered with grass and forests.

Ayers Rock

Frank Lane Picture Agency/Corbis

Roger Ressmeyer/© Corbis

Coral Island In Great Barrier Reef

Coastline Of The Cobourg Peninsula

Wayne Lawler; Ecoscene/Corbis

Dave G. Houser/Corbis

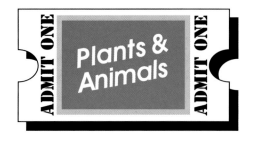

Koala On Kangaroo Island

Kevin Schafer/Corbis

Australia is known for its strange and beautiful creatures. In fact, many of the animals that live in Australia cannot be found anywhere else on Earth. Some animals are **marsupials**. Marsupials carry their young in pouches. Kangaroos, koalas, and wombats are all Australian marsupials.

Many kinds of snakes, fish, crocodiles, and birds live in Australia, too. Two important kinds of plants in Australia are the *eucalyptus* (yoo-kuh-LIP-tuss) and the *acacia* (uh-KAY-shuh). Acacia plants are often found in dry areas. Eucalyptus trees grow in wetter places. Many kinds of wildflowers also grow in Australia.

An Emu Can Be Taller Than A Car

Paul A. Souders/© Corbis

Kangaroo Near Alice Springs

Eric and David Hosking/Corbis

Alice Springs

Kangaroo Island • Hamilton

Eucalyptus Trees Near Hamilton

Port Jackson
Harbor
Around
1800

Arnhem
Land

NORTHERN
TERRITORY

QUEENSLAND

Port
Jackson

Long Ago

The first people to live in Australia were the **Aborigines** (a-buh-RI-juh-neez) They probably came to the continent from Southeast Asia. The Aborigines traveled in groups from place to place.

They hunted and lived on Australia's lands for thousands of years. In the 1600s, explorers from other countries began to arrive in Australia. They were searching for gold and good farmland.

Eye Ubiquitous/Corbis

Modern Aborigine From Arnhem Land

Late 1800's Northern Territory Aborigines

Hulton–Deutsch Collection/Corbis

Aboriginal Rock Painting From Queensland

Years later, some explorers from Great Britain told their king about Australia. He wanted it to be a part of his kingdom. The British took away the best land from the Aborigines. Great Britain ruled Australia for many years.

Michael Fogden & Patricia Fogden/Corbis

13

Australia Today

Today, Australia has its own government. It has its own flag and its own national song. But Australia still has many ties with Great Britain. Australians speak English and drink tea just as the British people do. And the Queen of Great Britain is still very important to many Australians.

Aboriginal people still live in Australia, too. But they often live in poor areas and cannot get very good jobs. To help, the government of Australia has set up programs for the Aborigines. These programs teach ways to become healthier, get better schooling, and find better jobs. Some programs even help Aborigines get their land back.

Paul A. Souders/© Corbis

Arnhem Land

Sydney

Canberra ☆

National Parliament House In Canberra

Busy
Railroad
Station In
Perth

MACDONNELL
RANGES

Perth

Lake
Macquarie

Surf Life
Savings
Championships

Paul A. Souders/© Corbis

Platform
6

About 18 million people live in Australia. Most of them live along the eastern and southeastern coasts. That is because the central parts of the country are too dry and hot. Many Australians are relatives of the British settlers.

Many others are **immigrants**, or newcomers from other countries. Aborigines still make up a small part of the population, too. Australians are very friendly people. They welcome new faces and love to smile. They also like to have fun!

Paul A. Souders/© Corbis

Coal Miner From Lake Macquarie

Paul A. Souders/© Corbis

Girls At Surf Life Saving Championships

Aborigine Cowgirl In The MacDonnell Ranges

Penny Tweedie/Corbis

ADMIT ONE

City Life
And
Country
Life

ADMIT ONE

Aborigine Camp In Arnhem Land

Penny Tweedie/Corbis

Almost all of Australia's people live in cities. These cities have shops, restaurants, and tall buildings just like those in the United States. But apartment buildings are very rare in Australia. That's because most people live in small houses called **bungalows**. Most bungalows have a yard and a garden for people to care for.

Australians call the countryside the *bush*. Some of the bush is very empty and lonely. This is known as the **outback**. Only a few people live there. To get around, people must use small planes.

That's because there are very few smooth roads in the outback. By flying planes, people can check on farm animals, look at crops, and even go to town for groceries!

People Live Underground In Coober Pedy

Paul A. Souders/© Corbis

Farmhouse in Victoria

Michael S. Yamashita/Corbis

Eye Ubiquitous/Corbis

Arnhem
Land

OUTBACK

Coober
Pedy

VICTORIA
Melbourne

The City Of
Melbourne

Students
At Lunch
In
Melbourne

Arnhem
Land

QUEENSLAND

Sydney
Melbourne

Paul A. Souders/© Corbis

Student At School Of The Air In Queensland

Patrick Ward/Corbis

Australian children start school when they are about five years old. They learn math, reading, science, and writing just as you do. But in the outback, students live too far away to attend regular schools. Instead, they learn through *correspondence schools* and *schools of the air*.

In correspondence schools, students receive and turn in their homework by mail. In schools of the air, teachers and students talk to each other on two-way radios!

Vietnamese Learn English In Sydney

Howard Davies/Corbis

English is the main language in Australia. It was brought over by the British settlers. Even today, the Australian language includes many British words. Australians also use Aboriginal words to describe things. "Koala" and "kangaroo" are both Aboriginal words.

Aborigine Girls Attend Mission In Arnhem Land

Penny Tweedie/Corbis

Work

Australians have all sorts of different jobs. Some people work in offices or in factories making paper or clothes. Others fish for lobsters, oysters, and shrimp. Still others work in the forests cutting lumber for building.

Shepherd North Of Boorowa

Paul A. Souders/© Corbis

But the best-known job in Australia is farming. The wide, open spaces of Australia's countryside are the perfect place for raising animals such as cattle and sheep.

The wool and meat from these animals can be sold to people all over the world. Many other Australian farmers raise apples, sugarcane, and wheat. These, too, are sold all over the world.

Cowboys From Victoria

Paul A. Souders/© Corbis

Opal Miner In Coober Pedy

Paul A. Souders/© Corbis

Coober
Pedy

Boorowa

VICTORIA

Farm In
Victoria

Hayman
Island
Resort
Restaurant

Darwin

Hayman
Island

Sydney

VICTORIA

Paul A. Souders/© Corbis

Cattleman Cooks Outdoors In Victoria

Australians eat many of the same foods we do. Meat, potatoes, and bread are all favorite dishes. Fresh vegetables and fruit are popular, too. And just like in the United States, Australians like foods from other countries. Italian, Greek, and Chinese dishes are all becoming popular in Australia.

Paul A. Souders/© Corbis

Cooking Noodles At A Market In Darwin

Cafe Entrance In Sydney Plaza

Paul A. Souders/© Corbis

Paul A. Souders/© Corbis

Pastimes

In Australia, people like to do many things. Some people like to watch television or visit with their friends. But most Australians like to do things outdoors. Surfing, swimming, tennis, golf, and boating are all favorite pastimes in Australia.

Team sports are also very popular. *Rugby* is one team sport that is very rough and dangerous. Players push and shove each other to get at a ball. Another sport, called *cricket*, is more calm. It is a little like American baseball.

Roger Ressmeyer/© Corbis

Camel Race At Alice Springs

Patrick Ward/Corbis

Australia III Yacht Off Fremantle

Lifeguards Compete Off Bondi Beach

Paul A. Souders/© Corbis

Alice
Springs

Fremantle

Bondi
Beach

Pakenham

Australian
Rules
Football
In
Pakenham

Darwin
Katherine

Sydney
Surf Carnival

Young Lifeguards
At Surf
Carnival

Patrick Ward/Corbis

Australians celebrate many of the same holidays we do. They also have special days of their own. One special holiday is *Australia Day*. It is celebrated every year on January 26. On this day, Australians remember when the first British settlers arrived in their country. With its fireworks and flags, Australia Day is a lot like the Fourth of July in the United States.

Charles & Josette Lenars/Corbis

Man Plays Dijeridoo At Ceremony In Katherine

Australia is known for its wide-open spaces, its bright sunshine, its strange animals, and its happy people. Perhaps one day you will visit this wonderful land. If you do, be ready for a good time—Australia is sure to make you smile!

Holiday Sunset At Darwin Beach

Sydney Opera House At Rest After Holiday

Paul A. Souders/© Corbis

Paul A. Souders/© Corbis

Aboriginal
Bark
Painting

Australia is really called "The Commonwealth of Australia." People just say "Australia" for short.

One famous song in Australia is called "Waltzing Matilda." But it is not about a girl who is dancing. The song is really a story about a wanderer.

The equator is an imaginary line that goes around Earth. Countries that lie above the equator have seasons at the same time as the United States. But Australia lies below the equator. It has its seasons at the opposite time. So when it is winter in the United States, it is summertime in Australia!

Just off the northeastern coast of Australia lies the Great Barrier Reef. It is a chain of more than 2,500 coral reefs. Many plants, fish, and ocean animals depend on the reefs for food and shelter.

How Do You Say?

	AUSTRALIAN SLANG	HOW TO SAY IT
Hello	g'day	guh-DAY
Friend	mate	MAYT
What?	Ay?	EYE
Oh my!	Blimey!	BLY-mee
No problem	no worries	no WUH-reez
Thank you	ta	TAH
See you later	hooroo	HOO-roo
Australia	Oz	AWZ

Glossary

Aborigines (a-buh-RI-juh-neez)
Aborigines were the first people to live in Australia.

bungalows (BUNG-guh-lowz)
A bungalow is a small house with one floor. Many Australian city-dwellers live in bungalows.

continents (KON-tih-nents)
Earth's huge land areas are called continents. Australia is a continent.

immigrants (IH-mih-grents)
Immigrants are newcomers from other countries. Many Australians are immigrants.

marsupials (mar-SOO-pee-ullz)
A marsupial is an animal that carries its young in a pouch. Koalas, kangaroos, and wombats are all marsupials.

outback (OWT-bak)
The outback is the empty, central area of Australia. Not many people live in the outback.

plateaus (pla-TOHZ)
A plateau is a flat area that is higher than the land around it. There are many plateaus in Australia.

Index

Aboriginies, 13, 14, 17, 18

animals, 10, 18, 22, 29

bungalows, 18

cities, 4, 18, 19

continents, 6, 13

farming, 9, 18, 22, 23

food, 25, 31

Great Britain, 4, 13, 14

holidays, 4, 29

immigrants, 17

land, 6, 9, 13, 14, 29

language, 4, 21

marsupials, 10

outback, 18, 21

pastimes, 26

plants, 10, 31

plateaus, 6

population, 4, 17

schools, 14, 20, 21

work, 22